WOMEN'S PRO BASKETBALL TODAY

THE HISTORY OF THE PHOENIX
MERCURY

SRAMVD OLLAR

WILSON IMC
OWATONNA MN 55060

Published by Creative Education
123 South Broad Street, Mankato, Minnesota 56001
Creative Education is an imprint of The Creative Company

Design by Stephanie Blumenthal
Cover design by Kathy Petelinsek
Production design by Andy Rustad

Photos by: NBA Photos

Library of Congress Cataloging-in-Publication Data

Dollar, Sam.
The History of the Phoenix Mercury / by Sam Dollar.
p. cm. — (Women's Pro Basketball Today)
Summary: Describes the history of the Phoenix Mercury professional
women's basketball team and profiles some of their leading players.
ISBN 1-58341-015-5

1. Phoenix Mercury (Basketball team)—Juvenile literature. 2. Basketball for women—
United States Juvenile literature. [1. Phoenix Mercury (Basketball team)
2. Women basketball players. 3. Basketball players.] I. Title. II. Series.

GV885.52.P46D65 1999   99-18891
796.323'64'0979173—dc21   CIP

First Edition

2 4 6 8 9 7 5 3 1

When eight cities were selected to be homes to the charter teams of the Women's National Basketball Association in 1996, Arizona fans were thrilled to hear Phoenix's name on the list. Since that time, the rowdy Phoenix Mercury fans—dubbed the "X factor" for the role they play in firing up the home team—have had a lot to cheer about, including two postseason appearances. America West Arena, the floor where Mercury players and fans come together to take on all challengers, has become one of the most feared places in the WNBA for visiting teams. With such stars as Jennifer Gillom and Michele Timms lighting up the desert sky, Mercury fans will continue to shake the arena for years to come.

THE X FACTOR: FANS AT

AMERICA WEST ARENA

SHOW THEIR SUPPORT.

MILLER DRIVES THE RISING MERCURY

Even though talented players like Jennifer Gillom and Michele Timms would be assigned to the Mercury before the 1997 season, Phoenix management knew that it would take excellent coaching for those players and the rest of the roster to reach their potential. Arizona basketball fans considered themselves lucky when Cheryl Miller—arguably the greatest female basketball player who has ever laced up a pair of high tops—was hired as head coach.

Miller's honors and achievements speak for themselves. In 1995, she became only one of 11 women inducted into the Naismith Memorial Basketball Hall of Fame. She was the national college player of the year three years in a row at the University of Southern California and became the first USC player to have her number retired. The standout guard also led the United States' women's team to a gold medal in the 1984 Olympics and later led the U.S. to titles in the World Championship of Basketball and the Goodwill Games.

But Miller wasn't only a great player; she had also proven herself as an outstanding coach at USC for two seasons after her playing days, piling up 44 wins and losing only 14 games. In 1994, Miller's team won the Pacific-10 Conference title.

HEAD COACH CHERYL MILLER

She then left the college sidelines to be a basketball analyst and National Basketball Association reporter. During her short broadcasting career, however, she realized that she wanted to coach again. "You're learning so much," she said of her work as an analyst, "[and] you're able to sit there and talk shop with [analysts] Hubie Brown and Chuck Daly and [NBA coach] Danny Ainge. . . . And they get you so excited about the game itself. . . ."

This passion for learning about the game fueled Miller's desire to coach at the professional level. "I spent a season and a half at USC," she said, "and it was a great experience for me, but it certainly wasn't an opportunity for me to really sharpen my teeth and do what I would have liked."

Miller, known throughout basketball circles as a great motivator, came to the Phoenix franchise with the same fierce attitude that made her an excellent player and college coach. Like the Mercury's fans, the thing Miller set her sights on from her first day on the job was a WNBA championship.

THREE VETERANS, ONE POTENT OFFENSE

Part of the reason the Mercury have been so tough for two seasons is that they have a core group of veterans at the top of their games: Michele Timms, Jennifer Gillom, and Bridget Pettis. Between them, the three have 35 years of playing experience that includes competition at the college, Olympic, and professional level.

Michele Timms got her start playing basketball in Australia, where "there was always a game going on in the backyard."

But she never dreamed of playing professionally, because there weren't any women's leagues when she was a youngster. Instead, she decided to become a physical education teacher. It wasn't until after the 1988 Olympics that she joined a pro team in Germany, becoming the first Australian—man or woman—to play professional basketball outside of Australia.

The key to Timms's success as a point guard has always been her leadership ability on the floor. In addition to being a great outside shooter—with a career three-point percentage of .46—she creates countless scoring opportunities for others with assists, a skill that does not go unnoticed by her teammates. "For me it's easy because she gets me so many good passes, and I just get them into the basket," said Marlies Askamp, the Mercury's 6-foot-5 center. "She puts everything together; she's the head of our team."

Although capable of dominating games with her potent offense, it is her defensive play that Timms is most proud of. "It's a trait of Australians to play good, aggressive defense," she said. "We [give] each other five after a steal rather than [after a basket]." Although few things upset her as much as an opponent beating her off the dribble for a basket, not many players get by the defensive stopper, as indicated by her 2.63 steals-per-game average in 1997.

Jennifer Gillom—nicknamed "Grandmama" as the Mercury's oldest player—also became interested in basketball at a young age. Her love for the game led her from the hoops in her family's cow pastures to the floor at the University of Mississippi,

ASSISTS LEADER

MICHELE TIMMS (ABOVE);

UMEKI WEBB (LEFT)

CO-CAPTAIN JENNIFER GILLOM

where she wowed basketball fans in the mid-1980s. Her spectacular college career included 2,186 points—placing her second on the school's all-time scoring list behind her older sister Peggie—1985 Basketball Sportswoman of the Year honors, and All-American honors, among other awards.

Even after playing 12 professional seasons, the Grandmama of the league shows no sign of slowing down. The Mercury's center finished the 1998 season averaging more than 20 points per game and became only the second player in WNBA history to surpass the 1,000-point mark. "I've always had confidence," Gillom said after the career season, "but I don't think I've ever believed in myself as much as I have this season."

In addition to her renowned steady play, Gillom has earned a reputation as an unparalleled performer in clutch situations. In three games in the Mercury's short history, she has scored with less than one second left on the clock to either win the game or send it into overtime. This "buzzer-beater" role is one that she thrives on. "Actually, I don't feel like there's any pressure," she said. "I've been playing that role for a long time now. . . . I like to be the 'go-to' man." Since Gillom—who turned 34 during the 1998 season—feels she has at least two or three more good years left in her WNBA career, Phoenix fans can count on more of her last-second heroics in the seasons ahead.

Phoenix's powerful veteran threesome is rounded out by

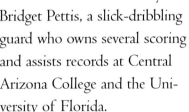

Bridget Pettis, a slick-dribbling guard who owns several scoring and assists records at Central Arizona College and the University of Florida.

DENA EVANS (ABOVE);

MIKIKO HAGIWARA WAS

IN THE FIRST TRADE OF

WNBA HISTORY (BELOW).

NAME: Cheryl Miller

BORN: January 3, 1964

POSITION: Head Coach/General Manager

SEASONS COACHED: 1997-present

RECORD: 37-25

As a player at USC, Miller enjoyed back-to-back national titles in 1983 and '84 and earned All-American honors four straight seasons. In 1993, she returned to USC as head coach, compiling a 44-14 record and one Pac-10 conference title in two seasons. In 1997 Miller joined the Mercury staff and led her squad to a 16-12 (.571) regular season before they were beaten by New York in the first round of the playoffs. The following year, Miller took her team to the next level: the WNBA championship game. Phoenix finished the season 19-11 before downing Cleveland 2-1 in the semi-finals and finally falling to Houston in the finals. Miller's Mercury teams have emphasized defensive ball pressure to create turnovers.

NAME: Jennifer Gillom

BORN: June 13, 1964 (Abbeville, Miss.)

POSITION: Forward/Center

HEIGHT: 6-foot-3

COLLEGE: Mississippi '86

AWARDS AND HONORS: All-WNBA First Team 1998, Player of the Week 7-6-98, All-WNBA Second Team 1997, Player of the Week 8-11-97, team co-captain

Gillom, known to WNBA fans as "Grandmama," has had a history of game-winning shots, including a lane jumper in Game One of the 1998 Championship series. The veteran forward led her teammates in scoring both seasons and finished second in league scoring in 1998. Her season-high 36 points against Cleveland in 1998 was also a league best.

STATISTICS: 1,064 career points

Year	Average	Total Points	Avg. Rebounds
1997	15.7	440	5.4
1998	20.8	624	7.3

PORTRAIT

13

Pettis's consistency and intensity on the court make her an invaluable asset to the Mercury. The 5-foot-9 guard finished the 1998 season averaging 11.3 points, 3.4 rebounds, and 2.1 assists per game. Perhaps her most remarkable feats have come at the foul line: her 1997 free-throw percentage was near 90 percent; in 1998, it dropped minimally to 86 percent (the third highest in the WNBA). Pettis credits her success less to her superior ability than to her attitude. "Always believe in yourself," she said, "and you will succeed."

INTERNATIONAL PLAYERS ADJUST IN THE STATES

Few teams in the WNBA have as many international players as Phoenix. The Mercury roster includes six players from overseas, including three from Australia: Michele Timms, guard Kristi Harrower, and forward Michelle Griffiths. Slovakian guard Andrea Kuklova, 6-foot-5 German center Marlies Askamp, and 6-foot-8 Russian center Maria Stepanova round out Phoenix's international roll call.

Such diversity can create difficulties, since foreign players often describe the American style of basketball as faster-paced and more physical than many foreign styles, which tend to emphasize

RELIABLE SCORER BRIDGET PETTIS

strong fundamentals. To blend contrasting approaches from player to player, the Mercury spent a lot of time from the start of their 1997 training camp working on helping all players jell together as a team.

One player who has shown no trouble adjusting to the U.S. game is Michelle Griffiths, a forward from Australia. She was assigned to the Mercury in May 1998 after playing professionally for eight years in Australia and helping Team Australia win a bronze medal in the 1996 Olympics.

Although few fans could find flaws in her play in her first year with the Mercury, she admits that it took her a while to become comfortable with her game. "In Australia, we play the Australian way," she said. "So coming to America, I have had to learn the American style of play. It has been very hard, but I have learned to be patient, and we as a team have learned that basketball is an international language—you just have to score to win."

Griffiths made great strides in her game in 1998, finishing the season averaging 9.2 points and 4.4 rebounds per game, but her teammates knew that she was a critical part of their success from day one. "Michelle has done a tremendous job for this team," Gillom said. "She gives 100 percent every game and has taken a lot of pressure off of me. She started playing well from the beginning of the year."

But Griffiths wasn't the only foreign talent adding to the Mercury's offensive punch. Although playing limited minutes off the bench, Askamp, Kuklova, and Harrower would also make valuable contributions. The three combined for nearly 11 points per game in 1998, as Askamp showed promise as a rebounder, Kuklova proved her versatility, and Harrower showed an accurate shooting touch from the outside.

As they get more comfortable as a team and continue to adapt to the American style of play, Griffiths and her international teammates will continue to give Phoenix fans something to cheer about and opposing teams something to fear.

A SHOT AT A DREAM

When the WNBA's first season began, Mercury fans felt certain that their team would be going to the finals. America West Arena was packed game after game, the fans gave their team full support, and the Mercury were playing some of the best basketball in the league.

The Mercury started off with an impressive 8–3 record, plowing through the competition. Timms and Gillom spearheaded the offensive attack early, but

BRANDY REED (ABOVE)

AVERAGED 5.2 POINTS IN

1998; MARLIES ASKAMP

(BELOW)

the Mercury also received welcome contributions from forward Toni Foster, who twice led the team in scoring. Phoenix would then struggle, however, losing six games in a row. The Mercury's previously-great defense, which had held opponents to less than 60 points in six of the first nine games, fell apart as opponents rolled to an average of 77 points per game.

But behind the steady leadership of the Mercury's big three—Timms, Gillom, and Pettis—Phoenix righted the ship to go 8–4 the rest of the way and finish their first season at 16–12. An overtime victory over the Los Angeles Sparks on August 24 gave the Mercury the Western Conference crown and a playoff berth against the powerful New York Liberty.

During the regular season, Phoenix played New York four times, winning twice at America West and losing both games in Madison Square Garden. The teams' fifth meeting—a one-game semi-finals contest—would decide who moved on to the finals. Even though the Mercury felt good about their chances at home against New York, they knew that it would be a battle. "We're not getting over-confident because we're at home, that's for sure," said Timms. "We want to make sure we get the job done, not only for ourselves and the coaching staff, but also for the people of Phoenix."

The game started with tough defensive efforts by both sides, and the Mercury trailed by only five points at halftime.

Unfortunately, poor shooting early in the second half cost the Mercury dearly, as the Liberty ran away to a 59–41 blowout win. Although Phoenix posted its lowest scoring output of the year in the season's biggest game, Coach Miller accepted the loss with dignity. "In a game of this magnitude, you have to bring your 'A' game," she explained. "Sometimes the shots fall—sometimes they don't."

The loss was certainly a bitter pill to swallow, but Mercury fans and players alike knew that they had a lot to be proud of. With this attitude, Phoenix went into its first off-season with big plans for 1998.

CHAMPIONSHIP HEIGHTS

The 1998 season would start much the same way 1997 had for the Phoenix Mercury. Halfway through their schedule, the Mercury's record stood at a lofty 11–4. Gillom exploded from the gates, averaging an incredible 22.4 points per game in 10 team-leading performances. As the veteran continued her high-powered play, center Marlies Askamp and forward Brandy Reed quietly took their games to new levels, doing heavy damage on the boards and in the scoring column.

Unfortunately, the 1998 season would also mirror the mid-season losing skid of the year before, as the Mercury dropped five straight games late in July. But the Mercury would again finish the season strong, winning seven of their last nine games to drive themselves into the playoffs with momentum. The Mercury continued to rise as they beat the Rockers at Cleveland on August 25 to

BRANDY REED CAME ON STRONG IN THE FINAL 10 GAMES OF 1998.

PORTRAIT

NAME: Michele Timms

BORN: June 28, 1965 (Melbourne, Australia)

POSITION: Guard

HEIGHT: 5-foot-7

COLLEGE: Burwood College (Australia)

Team co-captain Timms led the Mercury in assists both seasons, finishing second in the league in 1997. The Australian National Team member's three-point numbers dropped off during the '98 regular season, but she gave Phoenix a boost in the playoffs, scoring a team-high 21 points against Houston in Game 2. The durable guard missed only one start in two seasons of play.

STATISTICS: 533 career points

Year	Average	Total Points	Avg. Assists
1997	12.1	326	5.1
1998	6.9	207	5.3

NAME: Bridget Pettis

BORN: January 1, 1971 (East Chicago, Ind.)

POSITION: Guard

HEIGHT: 5-foot-9

COLLEGE: Florida '93

Pettis thrived at the free-throw line in 1997, finishing as the league's top shooter at .898. Her numbers dropped slightly in '98 to .865, third-best in the WNBA. The Mercury's second-most prolific scorer posted a career-high 27 points and 11 rebounds in Game 3 of the WNBA semifinals against Cleveland. She averaged 12.8 points and 2 assists in the '98 playoffs.

STATISTICS: 690 career points

Year	Average	Total Points	Avg. Rebounds
1997	12.6	352	3.8
1998	11.3	338	3.4

PORTRAIT

capture the semi-finals series two games to one and earn the right to face the reigning WNBA champions, the Houston Comets, for the league title.

The Mercury were confident going into game one of the finals, having beaten the Comets on June 24 and taken them to the wire in a 65–62 loss on July 21. Game one of the series was also on Phoenix's home court in America West Arena, where more than 13,000 roaring fans gathered to watch the Mercury slay the Comets' dazzling trio of Cynthia Cooper, Tina Thompson, and Sheryl Swoopes.

The Mercury came out unintimidated by Houston's fearsome threesome. Although they trailed the champions 16–8 early, guard Andrea Kuklova came off the bench to score once, hand out three assists, and block one shot, boosting Phoenix to a four-point lead at the break. Kuklova's poised and patient play helped steady the Mercury's focus, and they hung on for a 54–51 victory. "It was a very important game, and I played well," the 6-foot Kuklova said afterward. "I played good defense, and on offense I didn't force anything and took my time."

After game one, Coach Miller said that game two would be a war. Her prediction proved accurate, and with eight minutes to play and her Mercury up by 12 points, it looked like Phoenix would win the war and the WNBA crown. But then something happened: rebounds started bouncing away from Phoenix players, and the Mercury's shots clanged harmlessly off the rim. While the Mercury went cold, Cynthia Cooper and Sheryl Swoopes stole the momentum to put together a scoring run to force the game into overtime. Having watched their double-digit lead fizzle away, Phoenix would come up five points short in the extra frame, 74–69.

Coach Miller, normally outspoken, adopted a calm attitude when facing the media after the game. "Seriously, did you not expect Houston to get back in the game?" she asked. "They're champions."

MIKIKO HAGIWARA

(ABOVE); GUARD

BRIDGET PETTIS (BELOW)

As Miller prepared her team for the final and deciding battle at Houston's Compaq Center, the pressure mounted. Phoenix, however, couldn't wait for the game to start. "We've shown when our backs are against the wall," said Michelle Griffiths, the Mercury's standout power forward, "we tend to get tougher and pull together."

The Mercury did come out playing tough, trailing by only six points at halftime and going on a 10–2 run in the second half to take the lead. With less than eight minutes to go, both teams continued to trade baskets. With under four minutes left to play, the Mercury were still within striking distance at only four points down. But a layup by the Comets' Janeth Arcain and four straight free throws by Sheryl Swoopes put the game out of reach.

Phoenix's dream season crumbled with the 80–71 loss, but the Mercury had proved that they could run with Houston's stars. Michelle Griffith finished the game with a career-high 24 points, while Gillom scored 20 points and Bridget Pettis added 13.

Although the Mercury players were disappointed with the loss, they had earned the respect of the Comets. "Phoenix was the one team that pushed our buttons and took us to the limit, and really showed what they're made of," Cynthia Cooper said. "They exploited our weaknesses. They were definitely a tough opponent."

Cheryl Miller was proud of her team's effort and optimistic for 1999. "I'm proud of this team," she said. "I don't think

PAULINE JORDAN (ABOVE);

CHERYL MILLER STRESSED

DEFENSE (RIGHT).

there's a coach in this league that has more respect or more admiration for his or her players."

OFF-SEASON OPTIMISM

Although many professional teams spend their off-seasons searching for ways to improve, the Phoenix Mercury's off-season was a quiet one after falling just nine points short of the WNBA championship. With Gillom, Timms, Griffiths, Pettis and a cast of young talents on the rise under the thumb of Cheryl Miller, Phoenix has the talent and the coach to make another strong run at the league championship.

What the Mercury have lacked in their first two seasons is an outstanding perimeter player, a player who can dominate a game by spreading the defense and shooting from the outside. Michele Timms had a sub-par scoring season in 1998, averaging only 6.9 points per game, and Andrea Kuklova—who has the potential to become a premier scorer—has not gotten enough playing time to develop her skills. As Gillom said after the finals, "We lack a shooter, and it showed."

To fill the void, the Mercury will look to their roster of young, talented players capable of providing the necessary offensive spark. Phoenix management hopes that such

ANDREA KUKLOVA HAS

SCORING POTENTIAL

(ABOVE); BRANDY

REED (BELOW)

youngsters as guards Umeki Webb and Kristi Harrower, both just 23 in 1998, develop into offensive leaders down the road.

Another key to the team's future offensive success is Maria Stepanova, the Mercury's 6-foot-8 center and the youngest player on the team at 19. Despite her youth, Stepanova played professionally in Russia for three seasons before joining the WNBA, averaging 15.9 points and 12.4 rebounds during the 1997–98 season. At 17, she became the youngest member of the 1996 Russian Olympic team.

Although Stepanova played well in her first WNBA season, she averaged only about six minutes of playing time per game while Jennifer Gillom did most of the team's work at the center position. But with her remarkable size (she's the second tallest player in the WNBA) and natural ability, Miller knows that Stepanova could be dominant as a rebounder and shot-blocker: a presence the Mercury need almost as badly as they need an outside shooter. "The opportunities are endless for Maria," said Coach Miller.

Stepanova's physical skills will certainly improve with each season, but the Phoenix coaching staff has been most amazed by her mental toughness and instincts for the game. "Physically, you can't expect a whole lot from a 19-year-old, because she's still growing into her body," Miller said. "It's the mental part I'm excited about. I'm telling you, the kid is so dang amazing."

6-FOOT-8 CENTER MARIA STEPANOVA

While the Mercury's young guns work on their games in the off-season, many of the team's veterans continue to play overseas during their time off from the WNBA, honing the skills that they hope will put them over the top in the upcoming season. Michele Timms spent the off-season playing in Australia, while Gillom dazzled fans in Istanbul, Turkey.

The future of the Phoenix Mercury is bright from every angle. The team has two winning seasons, two playoff appearances, and has come within one game of winning the league title. In Jennifer Gillom and Michele Timms, Phoenix has two of the game's greatest players. With their strong winning foundation, confident and talented players, and ever-supportive fans, the possibilities seem endless for the rising Mercury.